Contents

Secret attack

Place: Japan
Date: 1400s

A dark figure slips through the shadows. He finds his enemy and pulls out a star-shaped blade. He throws his weapon and his enemy is dead.

Is anyone safe from a ninja attack?

Ninja timeline

1400s	Many rulers in Japan use ninja to fight enemies
1550s	Ninja starts to lose power
1600s	People from Europe start to settle in North America
2000s	You are reading this book

Who were the ninja?

The ninja were trained killers, called **assassins**. Assassins went on special **missions** to kill or injure enemies. Ninja fought in Japan from the 1400s to the 1600s.

Where the ninja lived

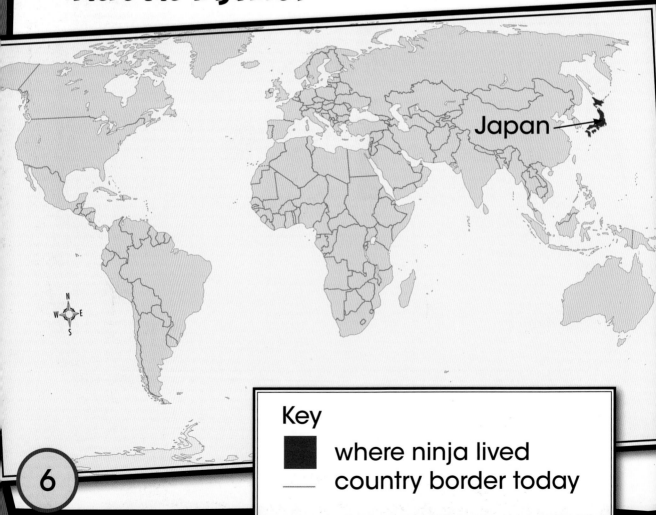

Japan

Key

█ where ninja lived

—— country border today

DID YOU KNOW?

Only people in special families could be ninja.

Becoming a ninja

Ninja families told their children the secrets of how to fight. Ninja children had to learn to be very tough. Children started training as soon as they could walk and talk. They learned to balance, jump, and hide.

You need to be able to balance well to do a ninja kick.

Older children learned to fight and
defend themselves. Teenagers learned
to use and hide special ninja weapons.
They had to be tough, fit, and silent.

DID YOU KNOW?
Ninja learned how to creep up on their enemies without anyone hearing.

Female ninja

Women could be ninja too. Women ninja were called *kunoichi* (say *koo-no-ee-chee*). Women ninja could use their beauty to get close to a **victim**. Then it was easy to kill him.

DID YOU KNOW?

Kunoichi often pretended to be servants or dancers in an enemy's home to get close to him.

13

Ninja missions

Ninja were like spies. Rulers used ninja to get information about their enemies or to kill them. Ninja could work quickly and silently. Often it was hard for people to know what had happened.

Rulers like this would have hired ninja to spy for them.

DID YOU KNOW?

People told stories that ninja could walk on water and through walls. This made their enemies very scared!

Some rulers in Japan lived in castles like this.

Ninja had leaders called *jonin* (say *joe-neen*). Often ninja did not know who their *jonin* was. This meant the ninja could not tell their enemies where they lived.

Sometimes ninja disguised themselves as farmers.

Do you think this may be a secret ninja village?

DID YOU KNOW?

Ninja lived in secret villages away from other people until it was time to go on a **mission**.

Ninja weapons

A ninja's best weapon was his or her fists. They learned to fight quickly and trick their enemies. They also fought with chains, sticks, and swords.

Ninja also had special weapons that they could hide. They threw star-shaped knives at their **victims**. They even hid darts in their mouths that they could blow into their enemy's eyes.

shuriken - throwing star

Ninja were experts with many different weapons.

Ninja skills

Ninja could hide in shadows and seem invisible. They used disguise so people couldn't recognise them. They walked in special ways so nobody could hear them coming.

DID YOU KNOW?

Ninja even stayed downwind from their enemies so dogs couldn't smell them.

Ninja used different skills when they were spying. They lived among their enemies and gathered information. They told their enemies lies to confuse them.

DID YOU KNOW?

Ninja built secret escape tunnels in case they were found spying.

The end of the ninja?

When the rulers in Japan stopped fighting there was no need for the ninja. Some ninja became **outlaws** and some became police. Ninja have become famous in stories, cartoons, and films.

The characters in Teenage Mutant Ninja Turtles use some of the skills that ninja used.

Ninja activity

Can you move as silently as a ninja?
Try these ninja **stealth** moves:

Move like a crane

Move slowly. Lift your knees high and point your toes as you place your foot on the ground. Ninja used this move to walk through shallow water or dry leaves.

Move like a crab

Bend your knees and move sideways quickly. Ninja used this move to sneak through shadows and passageways.

Move like an octopus

Crouch down and slowly bring your back foot forward. Point the toes of this foot and feel the ground in front of you before putting it down. Then repeat with the new back foot. Sweep your hands in and out as you do this.

Glossary

assassin person who murders others, often on orders

defend protect from danger or attack

mission special task, often secret

outlaw person who goes against the law

stealth secret or quiet

victim person who is attacked or hurt

Find out more

Books

Combat Sports: Karate, Clive Gifford
(Franklin Watts, 2008)

Ninja, Jason Glaser
(Capstone Edge Books, 2007)

We're From Japan, Victoria Parker
(Heinemann-Raintree, 2005)

Places to visit

The British Museum, London
www.britishmuseum.org/

You can find out more about Japanese history in the
Japan Gallery at the British Museum.

Find out

Can you find out
about the clothes
ninja wore?

Index